✔ KU-575-675

# Secret Agents

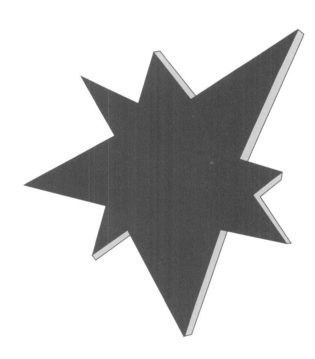

## by Paul Thomas

Belitha Press

L 46192

640056 SCH

JBC

First published in 2002 in Great Britain by
Belitha Press,
an imprint of Chrysalis Children's Books plc.
64 Brewery Rd
London N7 9NT

Copyright in this format © Belitha Press 2002
Text copyright © Paul Thomas

ISBN 1 84138 4550

Printed by Midas, Hong Kong

Editor: Christine Hatt
Series designer: Hayley Cove
Picture researcher: Diana Morris
Consultant: Hazel Mary Martell

All rights reserved. No part of this book may be reproduced or utilized in
any form or by any means, electronic or mechanical, including photocopying,
recording or by any information storage and retrieval system, without
permission in writing from the publisher except by a reviewer who may
quote brief passages in a review.

Photographic credits
AKG, London:11t, 24t, 30, 31b, 32t, 33, 36b, 43t, 43b.
Bridgeman Art Library: 7b British Library; 12 Private Collection; 14 Anne Brown
Military Academy, Providence, R.I.; 23t The Fine Art Society, London; 23b Christies,
London; 27b Novosti. Collections: 9b Brian Shuel. Corbis-Bettmann: 18, 19b, 20, 21b.
E.T. Archive: 35t. Mary Evans Picture Library: 11b, 19t, 21t, 25, 32b.
Hulton Getty Picture Collection: 6, 7t, 8, 9t, 22, 24b, 26, 27t, 28b, 29, 31t, 34,
36t, 37, 39t, 39b, 40b, 42, 44, 45t. Kobal Collection: 4 London Films.
North Wind Picture Archives: 15t, 15b, 16, 17t, 17b. Popperfoto: 5t, 10, 13t, 35b,
38, 41. Z. Radovan, Jerusalem: 45b.Rex Features: 5b, 28t Sipa/Tom Haley; 40t.

Words in **bold** appear in the glossary on page 46.

# CONTENTS

# INTRODUCTION

Throughout history, rulers, governments and armies have sent undercover agents to spy on their enemies. Some spies were motivated by greed, but others believed they were fighting evil.

## The first spies

One of the earliest undercover agents was Guy Fawkes. He attempted to blow up the English king James I and his parliament in 1605. In the late seventeenth and early eighteenth centuries, Daniel Defoe, more famous as the author of *Robinson Crusoe*, spied for Queen Anne and King George I.

## Undercover in America

In America, too, undercover agents made their mark. During the American Revolution, soldier Benedict Arnold sold his country's military secrets to Britain. In the nineteenth century, Harriet Tubman helped slaves escape to the northern USA.

## War work

The two major wars of the twentieth century provided numerous opportunities for undercover work. The glamorous Mata Hari was a spy during the First World War (1914-18), while many agents opposed the **Nazis** in the Second World War (1939-45).

An atmospheric scene from *The Third Man*, a film about spies in Austria after the Second World War.

The French Resistance worked undercover to locate German troops.

## Anti-Nazi plots

In Germany, Claus von Stauffenberg plotted to assassinate Nazi leader Adolf Hitler. In Hungary, Raoul Wallenberg helped the Jewish victims of the Nazis escape. In Yugoslavia, Tito organized **guerrilla** bands to ambush the Germans, while in France, Odette Churchill worked with the **resistance** against the enemy.

U-2 and ER-2 spy planes of the United States Air Force fly over San Francisco's Golden Gate Bridge.

## The Cold War

After the Second World War, spying increased as **Communist** and non-Communist countries tried to find out one another's secrets. This political struggle is known as the **Cold War**. One famous spy of the period was Kim Philby, who gave British secrets to the Soviet Union.

## All change

Today, sophisticated satellites and spy planes can reveal some secrets, for example about troop movements, from above the ground. As a result, the role of the spy has changed. But there will always be a place for the person who, with cunning and skill, can discover information that governments and individuals would much rather hide.

# GUY FAWKES

**1570–1606**

Guy Fawkes was one of the first undercover agents whose deeds have been recorded. In early seventeenth-century England, which was ruled by the **Protestant** king James I, he risked his life to fight for the rights of fellow **Roman Catholics**.

In 1534, following the Pope's refusal to grant him a divorce, the English king, Henry VIII, broke away from the Roman Catholic Church. He then made himself head of the Church in England. Henry remained a Catholic, but never again accepted the Pope's authority. He persecuted and even executed Catholics who would not accept him as Supreme Head of the English Church.

## Protestant and Catholic

Following Henry's death in 1547, the situation changed. The ideas of the **Reformation** grew popular and many people became Protestants. During the reign of the Protestant queen Elizabeth I (1558-1603), anti-Catholic feeling spread. After her death, the Protestant James I became king. As he was the son of the Catholic Mary Queen of Scots, many Catholics hoped for better treatment. But James let their persecution continue.

Guy Fawkes, the Catholic conspirator who almost blew up parliament in 1605.

The group of men who hatched the Gunpowder Plot to kill James I. Guy Fawkes is third from the right.

## Guy Fawkes

Guy Fawkes was born in York in 1570. He was brought up as a Protestant until his father died in 1579. Then his mother married a Catholic, and Fawkes adopted his stepfather's religion. During the sixteenth century, Catholic Spain ruled the Netherlands, whose Protestant people were fighting for independence. In 1593, Fawkes left England to join the Spanish army.

## Return to England

In 1604, a year after James I became king, Fawkes was asked to come back to England by fellow Catholic Thomas Winter. On his return, he saw how badly Catholics were treated and decided to do something about the situation. A suitable opportunity soon arose. During a meeting at the house of another Catholic, Robert Catesby, he was invited to join a plot to assassinate James I.

## The Reformation

In 1517, a monk called Martin Luther pinned a list of complaints to a church door in Wittenberg, Germany. He was angry about the wealth and power of the Roman Catholic Church. Many people supported him, and they became known as Protestants. Some Protestants destroyed statues in Catholic churches (below) as they believed them to be **idols**. The movement that Luther began is known as the *Reformation* because he wanted to *reform* the Roman Catholic Church.

## The Gunpowder Plot

The group decided that the only way to stop anti-Catholic persecution was to blow up the king and his parliament with gunpowder. They agreed to do this on 5 November 1605, when James I was to open the new parliamentary session. This Catholic conspiracy later became known as the Gunpowder Plot.

## Tunnel trouble

The plotters rented a house near the parliament buildings, then tried to dig a tunnel through to their cellars. But this was more difficult than expected because the walls of the house were extremely thick. So instead, Catesby found a cellar to rent directly underneath parliament, and the group hid the gunpowder there.

## Cellar keeper

Guy Fawkes agreed to look after the cellar and to light the fuse that would set off the explosion. He hid the gunpowder under firewood and coal. Then, adopting the name of John Johnson, he pretended that his job was to look after the piles of fuel.

Seated on his throne and dressed in his royal robes, King James I directs a meeting of parliament.

## Bonfire Night

On the night of 5 November 1605, people loyal to James I celebrated the failure of the Gunpowder Plot by lighting bonfires. Some made straw figures of Guy Fawkes and burnt them on top of the fires. To this day, people still burn a 'guy' and let off fireworks on 5 November. Children also sing:

*Remember, remember,*
*The fifth of November,*
*Gunpowder, treason and plot.*
*I see no reason*
*Why gunpowder treason*
*Should ever be forgot.*

## Anonymous note

One plotter, Francis Tresham, discovered that members of his family would be at the opening of parliament on 5 November. He begged the other conspirators to postpone their plan, but they refused. Instead, they promised to warn Tresham's family two days before. But Tresham sent an anonymous note to his cousin, Lord Monteagle, telling him to stay away. Monteagle showed the king, who ordered a search of parliament on 4 November.

## Discovery and arrest

The **Yeomen of the Guard** searched the cellars twice. On the first occasion, they discovered only Guy Fawkes looking after his piles of firewood and coal. But when they returned at eleven o'clock that night, they found the gunpowder hidden underneath the fuel. Guy Fawkes was immediately placed under arrest.

Guy Fawkes laying a trail of gunpowder underneath parliament just hours before his capture.

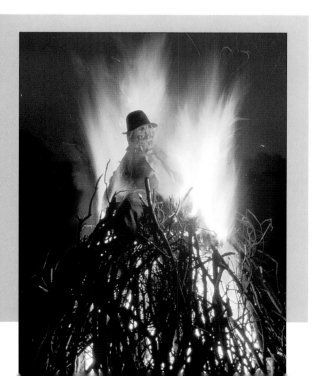

## Trial and execution

Guy Fawkes was tortured on the **rack**, but bravely refused to give away the names of the other plotters. He signed a confession, and in January 1606 was tried, then **hanged, drawn and quartered**. Catesby and three other conspirators were killed resisting arrest, Tresham died in prison, and seven men were hanged along with Fawkes.

## A place in history

Guy Fawkes was a courageous man, who was prepared to die for his religious beliefs. He has become one of the most famous undercover agents in English history for his involvement in the Gunpowder Plot.

# DANIEL DEFOE

**1660–1731**

Daniel Defoe is among the greatest names in English literature. Today he is best known as the author of *Robinson Crusoe*, but he was also one of the British monarchy's finest secret agents.

Defoe was born in London in 1660. His original surname was simply 'Foe', but he changed it to the more fashionable 'Defoe' in about 1703. Defoe's father was a wealthy, hard-working butcher and **chandler**, who had his son trained to be a minister of religion. But Defoe decided against this career, and by 1683 had set himself up in business as a **hosiery** merchant.

## A second career

In the 1680s, Defoe started a second career as a writer on politics and religion. He was passionately opposed to the **Roman Catholic** king, James II, and in 1685 took part in the Duke of Monmouth's rebellion against him. But he was an enthusiastic supporter of the **Protestant** William III, who replaced James in 1689. During these years, Defoe ran various unsuccessful businesses, but also spent much of his time writing pamphlets in favour of William.

Daniel Defoe led two separate lives. He was both a brilliant writer and a successful undercover agent for Queen Anne and later King George I.

People normally threw rotten fruit at criminals in the pillory. But they showered Defoe with flowers.

## Secret agent

While Defoe was in prison, his tile-making business collapsed and he was left with heavy debts. He appealed for help, and Robert Harley, Earl of Oxford, came to his rescue. Harley arranged his release on the understanding that Defoe would work for him as a pamphlet writer and secret agent. The earl thought Defoe would be highly suitable for the work because he was a trained and careful observer, who knew how to record all he saw and heard.

## The Glorious Revolution

When the Catholic James II fled Britain in 1688, parliament offered the throne to his daughter Mary and her husband William of Orange, a prince of the Netherlands. Both were Protestants. William and Mary invaded and became joint rulers. But William said he had no **divine right** to be king, and would only accept the position if parliament offered it to him. It did so in 1689 (below), and the monarchy became constitutional, that is subject to the law. This change in the relationship between Crown and Parliament is known as the Glorious Revolution.

## In the pillory

In 1703, Defoe got into serious trouble when he wrote a pamphlet that criticized the government. He was found guilty of **libel**, fined, imprisoned and forced to stand in the **pillory** three times. Defoe managed to turn his punishment into a triumph by writing a poem called *Hymn To The Pillory*. Many people bought copies. They also showed their support by covering Defoe's pillory with flowers and drinking his health.

## A new monarch

In 1702, William III died. Anne, Protestant daughter of the Catholic James II, then became queen. Anne's father had died a year earlier. But his Catholic son, James Stuart, was still alive in France. Many people, particularly in Scotland, thought he was the true heir to the throne.

## The Jacobite threat

The supporters of James Stuart were known as Jacobites, and they caused Queen Anne serious concern. So she decided to use Defoe, who supported her, to collect evidence against them. He later wrote that the queen had employed him 'in several honourable, though secret, services'.

## No hiding place

Defoe's role was to travel all over Britain, writing reports and listening to public opinion. He was particularly successful in discovering Jacobite hiding places. He even managed to spend time in their homes, where he listened to their conversations.

## Ambitious plan

The success of his undercover operations made Defoe a greatly respected figure in Queen Anne's court. So he wrote to Robert Harley with an ambitious plan to establish a new secret service, with more agents. Defoe believed this would allow the Queen's ministers to receive useful information from all parts of the country.

## Robinson Crusoe

At the age of 60, after producing many pamphlets on political and religious subjects, Daniel Defoe wrote *The Life and Strange Surprising Adventures of Robinson Crusoe of York, Mariner*, now known simply as *Robinson Crusoe*. This exciting tale of shipwreck and adventure on a tropical island was inspired by the true adventures of Alexander Selkirk, a Scottish sailor. It is regarded as the first English novel, and since its publication in 1719 has become one of the most famous and popular books of all time.

James Stuart, the son of the Catholic king James II. Jacobites believed he, not his sister Anne, should have become the monarch when William III died.

## Success and failure

The tour was the high-point of Defoe's career as a secret agent. The last years of his life were spent fighting legal battles over old debts. Historians believe that Daniel Defoe, the author of some of the most famous books in the English language, and perhaps the founder of the modern secret service, died hiding from his **creditors**.

The title page of Defoe's travel book (left). The book included maps of England, Wales and (below) Scotland. Perhaps Defoe used them to find secret Jacobite hide-outs!

## Tour of Britain

Following Queen Anne's death in 1714, George I came to the throne. During his reign, Defoe was even more successful. As the Jacobite threat continued to grow, he was sent on a tour of the kingdom to collect information. Defoe was now the king's main secret agent. He travelled under various **aliases**, and organized a network of agents directly answerable to him.

## Travel writer

During his travels, Defoe posed as a writer, and was able to uncover various groups of Jacobite rebels. But he did also write a successful book, *A Tour Thro' the whole Island of Great Britain*, published in 1726.

# BENEDICT ARNOLD

**1741–1801**

During the American Revolution, many famous people, including George Washington, fought to liberate their country from British rule. But a few Americans helped the British. Perhaps the most infamous of these traitors was Benedict Arnold.

Arnold was born into an important family in Norwich, Connecticut, in 1741. As a young man, he ran away to fight for the British in the **French and Indian War**. Then in 1762, after his parents died, Arnold moved to New Haven. There he set himself up as a **druggist**, bookseller and trader. He soon became a very wealthy man.

## The American Revolution

Arnold also became captain of a **militia** company. When the American Revolution started in 1775, he led his men to Fort Ticonderoga in New York, a British base. With the help of Ethan Allen, another militia leader, he captured the fort, and was made a colonel. Arnold then went to George Washington, the American commander, with a plan to invade Canada and capture the British post of Quebec. Washington agreed, and Arnold and 1100 men set out on the long march northwards.

Benedict Arnold sold American secrets to the British during the American Revolution.

## Failure and disappointment

After two months' marching, Arnold's exhausted soldiers arrived in Quebec. They launched an attack in December 1775, but were unable to capture the post. Arnold was wounded in the leg, but maintained a **blockade** around the city. He was made a brigadier general for his heroic efforts.

George Washington knew that Arnold was a superb commander and used him in several campaigns. But other commanders were jealous of Arnold's success, and they promoted a junior officer over his head. Arnold was furious at this treatment.

## Another battle

In 1777, Arnold was again in the thick of battle, at Saratoga, near New York, and managed to repel the British attack. But his horse was killed during the fighting, and he suffered a wound in the same leg that had been shot in Quebec.

### The assault on Quebec

Benedict Arnold's invasion of Canada took place in the bitter cold of winter. He marched his troops up through the state of Maine, then crossed the border and advanced on Quebec in a blinding snowstorm. There he met up with another American force under the leadership of the Irish-born general Richard Montgomery. But even their combined efforts were not enough to defeat the British forces. Arnold, though injured, lived to fight another day. Montgomery was killed during the attack, on 31 December 1775.

Fierce fighting between the Americans (in blue) and the British (in red) at Concord Bridge in 1775.

## Life in Philadelphia

Disabled from his wounds, Arnold was placed in command of the city of Philadelphia in 1778. He then started to live extravagantly and run up huge debts. This led him into corrupt business deals to raise money. At the same time, Arnold was becoming more friendly with families who supported the British. His first wife, Margaret Mansfield, with whom he had three sons, had died in 1775. In 1779 he married Margaret Shippen, the 18-year-old daughter of a pro-British American.

## The road to treason

The combination of family and financial pressures led Arnold to contact the British authorities. He hoped that they would pay for information about the American forces. Arnold told them about a planned American invasion of Canada, and gave away several other important military secrets.

## Major John André

Major John André was Benedict Arnold's British contact. On the night of 21 September 1780, Arnold met him to pass on the secrets of West Point's defences (right). But the following day, the Americans arrested André and charged him with spying. On 2 October 1780, the British soldier was hanged. A monument was erected to his memory in Westminster Abbey, London, where his remains are buried. He is the only spy ever to have been honoured in this way.

## West Point

Arnold also offered to surrender the military post of West Point in New York, of which he was commander. He asked for £20 000 and a job in the British army in return.

The city of Philadelphia, where Arnold became military commander in 1778.

## Exile in London

Arnold lived in London for 20 years. King George III welcomed him, but did not offer him an official post. Instead, Arnold earned his living by importing West Indian goods. Both he and his family were excluded from London social life because of his spying activities. Arnold died a bitter man in 1801.

## Notorious traitor

Benedict Arnold might easily have been remembered as one of the greatest commanders of the American Revolution. But thanks to a poisonous combination of resentment towards the army he served, extravagant living and personal greed, he is now much better known as one of his country's most notorious traitors.

## Discovery and flight

In 1780, Arnold's plan was detected by the Americans and he fled to the British side. He received only £6315 as financial reward for his treachery, but was made a brigadier general in the British army. Once in his new post, he led raids on the homes of many former friends. Arnold tried to persuade other Americans to join him, but only 28 were willing to desert. Following the British surrender in 1781, Arnold sailed to England with his wife and children.

Arnold escaped on horseback after his plot to surrender West Point was discovered.

# HARRIET TUBMAN

**1820–1913**

Harriet Tubman was born in 1820 on a plantation in the American South. She was given the name Araminta, but was known as Harriet, her mother's name. Like her parents, brothers and sisters, Harriet was a slave.

The plantation was a world in itself. The slave owner lived in 'the big house', as the slaves called it, while the slaves lived in 'slave row', a line of small cabins that were more suitable for animals than humans. Surrounding these were the cotton fields where the slaves worked. On the cotton plantations, slaves laboured in terrible conditions. They had no rights, and a slave owner could part a mother from her child or a husband from his wife at any time, simply by selling one of them.

## Early life

Harriet started work as a maid at the age of five. She looked after her owner's children until she was 12, when she was sent to work in the fields. A year later, Harriet tried to prevent a foreman from punishing one of the other slaves. He beat her so hard for interfering that he fractured her skull. Although she recovered, Harriet suffered from **black-outs** for the rest of her life.

Harriet Tubman escaped from slavery herself, then led hundreds of other slaves to freedom.

The comfortable and spacious 'big house' of a wealthy Mississippi plantation owner.

## Useful knowledge

Like most American slaves, Harriet never learned to read or write. But her father, Benjamin Ross, taught her how to find food and survive in the woods beyond the plantations. This knowledge was very useful to her in later years.

## Marriage and escape

In 1844, Harriet's owner let her marry John Tubman, a freed slave. Throughout their marriage, Harriet was afraid of being sold to a new owner in the Deep South. But her husband did not sympathize with her worries. In 1849, Harriet was about to be sold, but she escaped to Philadelphia in the North. She returned a few months later to find that her husband had remarried.

## The Cotton Kingdom

Before the nineteenth century, cotton-growing in the USA was limited to a few coastal states in the Deep South. This was because the only type of cotton that could be processed easily would not grow elsewhere. But in 1793, Eli Whitney invented the **cotton gin**, which made it possible to process plants that could grow inland. Gins were installed in many barns such as this (right) and cotton-growing spread rapidly westwards. The cotton-growing region became known as the Cotton Kingdom.

## The Underground Railroad

In 1850, Harriet returned to the South again to help her sister and two children escape to the North. A year later, she fetched her brother's family. All of them fled on the Underground Railroad, a network of road and sea escape routes between South and North. The Railroad was operated by ex-slaves, known as 'conductors'. The slaves were 'passengers', and the homes they hid in 'stations'. Harriet became a conductor and helped 300 slaves reach the North and Canada, where slavery was illegal. A $40 000 reward was offered for her capture.

## Fighting slavery

In the early 1850s, Harriet lived in Canada, where she acted as adviser to anti-slavery campaigner John Brown. In 1858, she moved to New York, but still worked hard for anti-slavery groups. In the 1860 elections, the anti-slavery candidate Abraham Lincoln became president.

## The American Civil War

The South wanted to keep slaves, so opposed Lincoln. Finally, some of the Southern states left the USA. This led to the American Civil War (1861-65), which the North won. Harriet was active in the Northern army as a nurse and spy. She commanded a group of soldiers that freed over 750 slaves. This was the only military campaign in American history to be led by a woman.

Harriet Tubman (far left) with some of the slaves she helped to escape.

House slaves waiting to be sold. They would soon be the 'property' of rich owners in New Orleans.

## After the war

In 1869, Harriet married Nathan Davies. The couple worked together for many years. They founded schools for freed slaves, where they taught and preached, raised funds for black people, and set up a home for the poor and elderly.

## Women's rights

Harriet also promoted the rights of black women and helped to found the National Association of Colored Women in 1896. At its first convention, she was enthusiastically congratulated for her bravery on the Underground Railroad and during the Civil War, as well as for her stand on women's rights. After a lifetime of hard work and struggle, Harriet died in 1913.

## The Moses of her people

Harriet Tubman was known by many names. The most famous was 'the Moses of her people' because, like Moses in the Old Testament of the Bible, she led slaves to freedom. Her ideals were summed up in this statement: 'There was one of two things that I had a right to, liberty or death; if I could not have one, I would have the other; for no man should take me alive...'

## Reconstruction

After the American Civil War ended, the Southern states had to be reunited with the USA. At the same time, former slaves and former slave-owners had to face up to a new way of life. The period in which all these changes took place is called Reconstruction (1865-77). At first, black people were helped to find work, build homes and study (right). The US **Constitution** was also changed to grant them equal rights. But gradually, white people took back power. It was to be many years before true change took place.

# MATA HARI

## 1876–1917

The most glamorous spy ever was Margarete Gertrud Zelle. She is remembered now as Mata Hari. Margarete was born in 1876 in Holland, the daughter of a merchant. She grew up to be a beautiful and adventurous young woman, with a great zest for life.

Margarete showed her sense of adventure at the age of 17, when she answered a **lonely hearts** advertisement. This was how she met her future husband, John MacLeod, a 38-year-old officer from the Dutch East Indies. The couple married and went to live in Java, an island in the Indian Ocean. Margarete was fascinated by the local customs, especially dancing.

## An unhappy marriage

Margarete soon realized that her decision to marry had been a mistake. Her husband drank too much. He also beat her and their children, a son who died while still very young, and a daughter. In 1901, the whole family returned to Holland. A year later, MacLeod deserted his wife and took their daughter with him. Margarete went to the courts and won **custody**. But her husband refused to support them, and soon mother and daughter were penniless. So Margarete had to leave her little girl with relatives.

Mata Hari in the costume of a Hindu princess.

## Javanese dancing

As a young woman in Java, Mata Hari watched the local female dancers. She was always excited by their elaborate and colourful costumes, especially the headdresses, which often included feathers and flowers. The women danced slowly, using their hands and eyes to emphasize different emotions. Mata Hari used these dancing styles when she worked in Paris in 1904.

The Folies Bergère was the most famous night club in Paris during Mata Hari's time in the city.

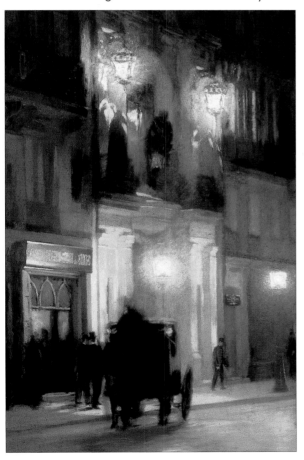

## A new life in Paris

By 1904, Margarete still had no money. But she remained adventurous, so decided to go to Paris in France. There she became an exotic dancer, using her knowledge of the dances she had seen in Java. It was at this time that she adopted the name Mata Hari, Malay words meaning 'eye of the day'.

Mata Hari was an enormous success and danced in France, Spain and Germany. She was praised as one of the most beautiful women in Europe, and many important men were rivals for her company. Over the next ten years, she had numerous lovers.

## The First World War

When the First World War started, in 1914, Mata Hari was living in Berlin. She had moved there to be with her companion, the German Chief of Police. He persuaded her to spy on the important men she knew. Any useful information she discovered was passed on to the German secret service. At the same time, Mata Hari was having a relationship with a captain connected to the French secret service and supplying confidential information to France.

## Test of loyalty

As a result of her double-dealing, no one trusted Mata Hari. Wherever she went in Europe, there was always a member of one or more secret services following her. She returned to France, but the French decided to **deport** her. Pleading with them for mercy, Mata Hari again offered her services as a secret agent. To test her loyalty, the French sent her on a mission to Brussels, the Belgian capital. There she was employed to spy on the occupying German forces.

A scene from the 1932 film *Mata Hari*, with Greta Garbo as the glamorous international spy.

## Code-breaking

Coded messages, often sent by **telegraph** operators like these in France (right), were widely used in the First World War. But the codes were frequently broken. The breaking of the code used in the 1917 Zimmermann telegram had dramatic consequences. The telegram was sent by the Germans to the Mexicans, asking them to enter the war by fighting the USA. British agents intercepted and decoded the telegram, then sent it to the American president, Woodrow Wilson. He told the American people what the telegram contained, and their outrage was one of the reasons why the USA entered the war.

## Caught in a trap

Despite her best efforts, Mata Hari could not get any information from her German contacts because of her reputation. So she travelled on to Holland and then by ship to Spain. When she arrived, German agents decided to betray her to the French. They deliberately sent a message to Spain using a code they knew the French had broken. In the message, the Germans ordered Mata Hari to return to France. She did so, making it clear to the French that she was still obeying German orders.

## Trial and sentence

Mata Hari was arrested in Paris on 13 February 1917 and charged with spying. Her trial lasted two days, and at the end she was sentenced to death. Many people appealed to the French government for mercy. But on 15 October 1917, Mata Hari was shot by a firing squad in Vincennes.

## Why did she die?

Historians believe that Mata Hari did not give the Germans information of any value. The French government knew this, so may have executed her only because she was an embarrassment. They may also have used her trial to distract attention from France's lack of success in the war at that time.

## Strange truth

The glamorous, headstrong Dutchwoman Mata Hari is one of the most famous undercover agents in history. Yet the strange truth is that she never passed on any important secret information at all.

This painting of Mata Hari's execution appeared on a book cover in 1917, the year of her death.

# TITO

Most undercover agents spend their whole lives working in secret. Yet the **Communist** and wartime **resistance** leader Tito eventually became the president of his country, Yugoslavia.

Tito's original name was Josip Broz. He was born in 1892 in Kumrovec, north-western Croatia, which at that time was part of the **Austro-Hungarian Empire**. Broz came from a poor peasant family and was the seventh of 15 children. At the age of 15, he was apprenticed to a locksmith in the town of Sisak. Later, as a young man, he was employed as a metalworker in Austria, Bohemia and Germany.

## The First World War

Travelling across Europe as a teenager, Broz saw how harshly working people were treated. He joined the Social Democratic Party of Croatia to fight against these injustices. But his plans to improve working conditions were stopped by war.

The First World War broke out in 1914, and Broz was **drafted** into the Austro-Hungarian army. He fought bravely and was given a medal for his courage. But in 1915, he was stabbed by a **Cossack**'s lance and captured by the Russian army.

Tito, the wartime resistance fighter who became premier and later president of Yugoslavia.

In 1915, during the First World War, Tito was wounded by Cossack troops like these.

## The Russian Revolution

During the Russian Revolution of 1917, Broz was released from prison. Inspired by this great Communist uprising, he too became a Communist. When he returned home to Croatia in 1920, he helped to set up the Communist Party of Yugoslavia.

## Communism in Yugoslavia

Broz started to work undercover to get his new party into power. As the Communist Party was an illegal organization in Yugoslavia, many other people worked for it outside the country. But Broz was quite different. He deliberately worked within Yugoslavia's borders. Gradually, he managed to gain support and organize the party on a national basis.

## New name

Broz also travelled to Moscow, Paris, Prague and Vienna to establish contacts with foreign Communists. At home and abroad he used **aliases** to disguise his identity. In 1928, he was imprisoned for his work. A year later he was released, and adopted one alias, Tito, as his own name.

## Communism

Communism is a political theory that was devised by German philosophers Karl Marx and Friedrich Engels. It states that property should be owned by the state rather than individuals, to bring about equality for all. Following a revolution in 1917 (below), the first country to adopt Communism was Russia (later called the Soviet Union). Some other countries freely adopted Communism, while more were forced to by the Soviets. In 1991, the Soviet Union broke up and many former Communist lands introduced democracy.

## The Second World War

Tito's talents as an undercover agent were used even more successfully during the Second World War (1939-45). On 6 April 1941, Germany invaded Yugoslavia. So Tito issued a proclamation calling all Yugoslavians to repel the **Nazi** invaders. Then he organized **guerrilla** bands to lead the fight. At first, these consisted of just a few men and women – the Partisans. Tito himself led them into battle against the Germans and their Italian allies.

## Ambush attacks

Tito soon gained military success by repeatedly ambushing the Nazis, then quickly retreating to the hills and woods. The Partisans won so many battles that the Nazi leader, Adolf Hitler, sent thousands of extra German troops to Yugoslavia to hunt them down and kill them.

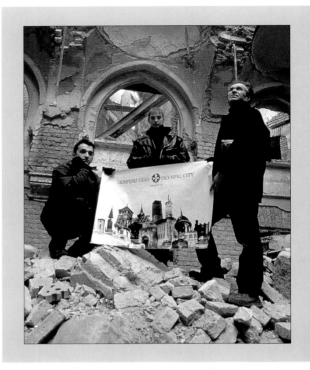

In this 1944 scene, wounded Partisans are transported by cart to hide-outs in the hills.

## The break-up of Yugoslavia

At the end of the First World War, in 1918, three **Slav** peoples living in south-east Europe, the Serbs, Croats and Slovenes, created a new country called Yugoslavia. They were ruled over by a Serbian king.

When the Second World War ended, in 1945, Yugoslavia became a **federation** of six republics, with Tito as ruler. When he died in 1980, the different Slav peoples each began to demand independence. In the early 1990s, fighting broke out, and three of the republics – Croatia, Slovenia and Bosnia-Herzegovina – finally broke away to form independent states.

Today much of the region lies in ruins. These inhabitants of Sarajevo (left) stand amid the rubble to recall the happier times of 1984, when their city hosted the Winter Olympics.

## Long struggle

Tito's guerrilla groups defeated the mighty German army. By 1944, he also had the support of the **Allies**. But thousands of Partisans died in the struggle. Tito himself was wounded and almost taken prisoner.

## From guerrilla to president

Tito became premier of Yugoslavia in 1945. Eight years later, he was elected president. Tito led Yugoslavia successfully for over 30 years, until he died on 4 May 1980, after a long illness. The young peasant from Croatia had become one of the most famous leaders in the world. Millions mourned his death and remembered his brave fight to keep Yugoslavia free and independent.

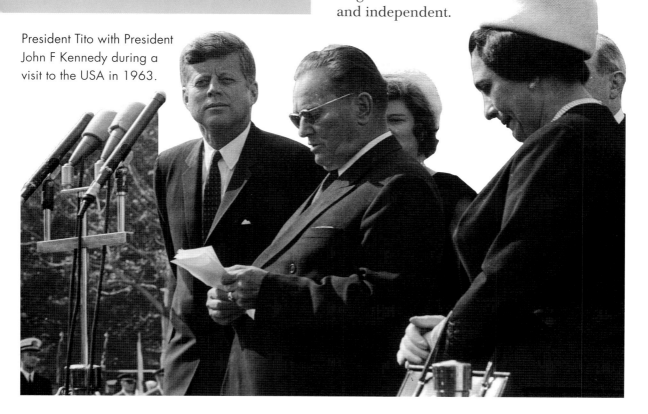

President Tito with President John F Kennedy during a visit to the USA in 1963.

# CLAUS VON STAUFFENBERG

**1907–1944**

As a member of an old and distinguished German family, Count Claus von Stauffenberg made a very unlikely conspirator. But he is famous as the man who almost killed Germany's notorious war leader Adolf Hitler.

Stauffenberg was born in November 1907 near Stuttgart in Germany. His family had worked in the royal courts for hundreds of years, and he could trace his ancestry back to the fourteenth century. As a boy, he went to the Ludwig Eberhard Gymnasium (grammar school) in Stuttgart. There he was taught that noblemen like him had a duty both to lead and to serve their country.

## Army training

After leaving school, Stauffenberg joined a top **Bavarian** cavalry regiment. He quickly established himself as a promising soldier, and was soon promoted to the rank of First Lieutenant. In 1936, Stauffenberg was sent on to the famous Berlin War Academy. His outstanding performance there meant that he would eventually be appointed to the General Staff, the group of senior generals who ran the German army.

Claus von Stauffenberg, a young officer who decided that Hitler had to die if Germany was to avoid defeat in the Second World War.

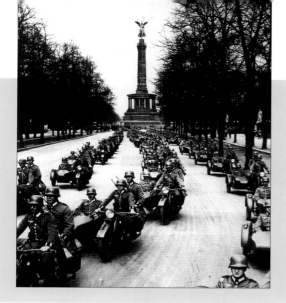

## The causes of the Second World War

When the First World War ended, in 1918, the victors (Britain, France, Russia and the USA) took over all Germany's pre-war territories. In the 1930s, the **Nazis** set out to recover them. Between 1936 and 1939, Germany invaded the Rhineland, Austria and Czechoslovakia. The British and French policy of **appeasement** allowed this. Then German troops massed in Berlin (left) and invaded Poland. Britain and France had warned this would mean war, and it was declared in September 1939.

## The Second World War

In the 1930s, Stauffenberg became very concerned that Germany was planning to go to war with the rest of Europe. In 1939, his worries were confirmed when Britain and France declared war on Germany because it had invaded Poland. This was the beginning of the Second World War (1939-45), which eventually involved most of the countries in the world. For the first three years of the war, Stauffenberg served in the Soviet Union, which was then Germany's ally. But in 1941, Germany declared war on the Soviet Union.

## Hitler must die

Stauffenberg believed that Germany could not win the war without Soviet help, so he became convinced that Hitler was leading his country to defeat. He was also growing extremely concerned at the brutality of Hitler's methods. In 1942, Stauffenberg decided that Hitler had to die. In the autumn of that year, he was heard to say: 'It isn't a question of telling the **Führer** the truth but killing him, and I'm ready to do the dirty work.'

The bad winter of 1942 forced the Nazis to leave the Soviet Union.

## Wounded in Africa

In January 1943, before he was able to make any plans, Stauffenberg was posted to North Africa. Three months later, he was wounded in an attack by an enemy plane. He lost his right hand, two fingers of his left hand and his right eye, and suffered injuries to his knee and ear. He was sent to Munich for medical treatment.

## The plot begins

Most officers who visited Stauffenberg in hospital agreed that Hitler should be assassinated. Without him, they believed, Germany could start peace negotiations with Britain and the Soviet Union, as well as the USA, which had entered the war in 1941. But the conspirators needed someone to get close enough to Hitler to kill him. This problem was solved in May 1944, when Stauffenberg became a **Chief of Staff**. His new post meant that he would have frequent access to Germany's leader.

Hitler greets one of his generals as Stauffenberg (far left) looks on.

## Adolf Hitler

Adolf Hitler, shown here saluting the Nazi army (left), was born in 1889. He fought in the First World War (1914-18), which Germany lost. In 1923, he wrote a book called *Mein Kampf* (My Struggle), which blamed the Jews for Germany's problems and stated that the country needed a strong leader. In 1933, he took on that role.

Hitler's ambition to conquer Europe led to the Second World War (1939-45), in which Germany was also defeated. Millions of people died as a result of the war, including six million Jews and others in **concentration camps**. Hitler escaped trial as a war criminal by committing suicide in his underground bunker in May 1945.

## The assassination attempt

The conspirators' plan was to place a bomb in a briefcase and leave it under the table at Hitler's headquarters in Rastenburg. Then Stauffenberg was to fly to Berlin, to set up a government. On 20 July 1944, Stauffenberg planted the bomb. It went off, killing four people, but Hitler suffered only bruises and burns. This was mainly because a wooden table leg had obstructed the explosion.

## Confusion and failure

Stauffenberg managed to reach an airfield and took off half an hour after the bomb exploded. But his fellow plotters in Berlin failed to act quickly. There was so much confusion about whether the German leader was alive or dead that the long-planned overthrow never even began.

## Arrest and death

At about ten o'clock that night, a group of officers who had remained loyal to Hitler arrested Stauffenberg and the other conspirators. A **court-martial** was quickly held and all the plotters were condemned to death. They were taken down to a courtyard and shot by a firing squad. As Stauffenberg fell to the ground, he shouted: 'Long live sacred Germany.'

The Second World War continued for another year, until Germany surrendered in May 1945. We can only guess how many lives would have been saved if Stauffenberg's plot had succeeded.

Nazi officers visit Hitler's headquarters after Stauffenberg's assassination attempt.

# KIM PHILBY

**1912–1988**

Harold Philby, known as Kim, became the most notorious and successful of the spies who met at Cambridge University during the 1930s.

Why do some undercover agents betray their own country? Often it is in the belief that their treachery will help their nation rather than harm it.

The most notorious group of agents to betray their country were the Cambridge spies – Guy Burgess, Donald Maclean, Kim Philby, Anthony Blunt and John Cairncross. They were all at Cambridge University during the 1930s, and believed that only the Soviet Union could stop the threat of the **Nazis** in Germany.

## Early life

The most famous member of this group was Harold Adrian Russell Philby. He was nicknamed 'Kim' after an Indian boy-spy in the novel of the same name by Rudyard Kipling. Philby was born in India in 1912. His father, Harry St John Philby, worked in the Indian Civil Service, although he later became a famous explorer. As a young man, Kim had a privileged education at Westminster School, London and Trinity College, Cambridge. Philby met Guy Burgess and Donald Maclean while at Cambridge, and like them was a strong supporter of Soviet Communism.

Philby developed his Communist ideas in student rooms like these in 1930s Cambridge.

## KGB recruits

The pro-**Communist** ideas of this group came to the notice of the KGB, the Soviet secret service, which recruited them as spies. The KGB believed these educated men would get good jobs, with access to information useful to the Soviet Union.

## War work

For Kim Philby, this proved to be true. The Soviets recruited him in 1933, and in 1939 he was appointed senior correspondent for *The Times* newspaper. In the same year, at the start of the Second World War, he was sent to France with the **British Expeditionary Force**. Then in 1940, British **intelligence** asked Philby to work for them. They wanted him to take particular responsibility for sabotage, **subversion** and propaganda. Philby had fooled them into believing that he was a patriotic Englishman, when all the time he was working as a Soviet spy.

## The Cold War

When the Second World War ended in 1945, a different kind of war started. This was the **Cold War**, a political conflict between the Soviet Union and its Communist allies in Eastern Europe, and the USA and its non-Communist allies in Western Europe. The conflict was symbolized by the Berlin Wall (right), which was built in 1961 and divided Communist East Berlin from non-Communist West Berlin. The wall was dismantled in 1989, and after the collapse of the Soviet Union in 1991, the Cold War ended and relations between the sides improved.

## Double agent

During the Second World War, Philby worked as a spy for the British and the Soviets. The British even wanted him to parachute into occupied Europe to spy for them. But Philby had a stammer. This was unsuitable for a spy on enemy territory, as it would make him stand out.

## After the war

In 1946, a year after the war ended, Philby was put in charge of British and American spying operations in the Soviet Union. The KGB were delighted because he was able to supply them with precious information at the same time as destroying information that might damage Soviet interests.

Like Philby, Guy Burgess (below left) and Donald Maclean were recruited by the KGB. Together they formed a highly successful spy network.

## MI6

In 1940, Kim Philby joined MI6, which stands for Military Intelligence, Section 6. Today this government agency is more often known by its alternative title, the Secret Intelligence Service. Its role is to work abroad gathering information about other countries, but it is based in this rather grand building in London (above). MI6's sister department, MI5, operates within the United Kingdom carrying out counter-intelligence. This is designed to prevent foreign governments spying here. MI5 is also involved in anti-terrorism work.

## Washington mission

Philby was trusted so much that he was sent to Washington, D.C., in the USA, three years later. His mission was to help the CIA, the American secret service, to spy on the Soviets, and to liaise between British and US intelligence. He was now one of the most important spies in the world. But an incident involving Burgess and Maclean soon changed the situation completely.

## Growing suspicions

Philby knew that the Americans suspected Maclean of spying, and in 1951 sent Burgess to London to tell him. Burgess warned Maclean, then both men escaped to the Soviet Union. This threw suspicion on Philby, as Burgess had been with him in Washington. For the next ten years, many people suspected Philby of spying for the Soviets. Although nothing could be proved against him, the suspicions alone meant that he had to leave his post in Washington and return to London. But he was soon spying for the British again in Cyprus.

## Final discovery

Eventually, Philby's luck ran out. In 1961, George Blake, another British spy working for the Soviets, was arrested. During his interrogation he named Philby as an agent. The authorities were so embarrassed by this discovery that Philby was not arrested.

## Flight to the Soviet Union

The British hoped that Philby would escape, to avoid the need for a trial that would publicly confirm people's suspicions. They were not to be disappointed. Philby fled to Moscow in 1961, and lived there until his death in May 1988. He continued to work for the KGB, and was buried in Moscow with full **military honours**.

## Betrayer or betrayed?

Like the other Cambridge spies, Kim Philby never regarded himself as a traitor to his country. He believed that Britain had betrayed him by not becoming a Communist country like the Soviet Union.

Kim Philby striding through Moscow in 1968. He lived in the Soviet capital for 27 years until his death in 1988.

# ODETTE CHURCHILL

**1912–1995**

Some of the bravest people to serve during the Second World War were undercover agents. These men and women volunteered for dangerous duties in occupied Europe. Among them was Odette Churchill.

Odette Churchill's original name was Odette Brailly. She was born in France in 1912, and educated at a convent school in Amiens. In 1931, Brailly married Roy Sanson, an English friend of her father's. The couple then moved to London, where they had three daughters.

## Going undercover

The Second World War began in 1939, and Odette's husband went away to serve in the armed forces. In 1942, Odette decided to move out of London with her daughters. Once settled in Somerset, she answered a government appeal for French speakers.

Nothing in Odette's background made it likely that she would become a secret agent. When she responded to the appeal, Odette thought she would be working as a translator. But the authorities recognized her courage and patriotism, and recruited her to carry out undercover work.

Frenchwoman Odette Churchill became one of the most courageous spies of the Second World War.

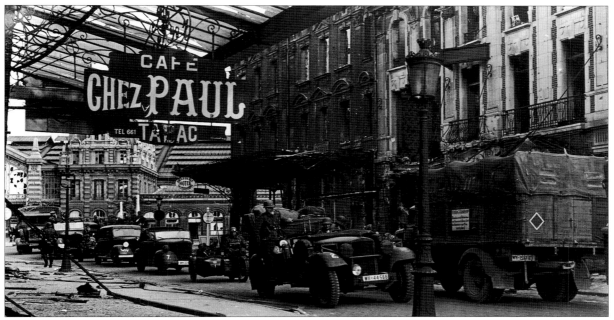

German troops arriving in the town of Arras,
northern France, in May 1940.

## The Gestapo

The Gestapo was the **Nazi** secret police force. It was originally made up of a small number of Hitler's personal bodyguards. But when he became **Führer**, the Gestapo grew bigger and more powerful. From 1936, it was led on Hitler's behalf by another high-ranking Nazi, Heinrich Himmler. These two Gestapo members (below) are arresting suspects in Berlin.

## A change of mind

Odette did not want to leave her children. But Germany had occupied part of France in 1940, and many people, including her own family, were suffering as a result. So she decided to go ahead. In October 1942, she landed in France and went to a safe house in Cannes. There she met Peter Churchill, the head of the local **resistance**.

## Communications courier

Odette worked as a courier for the resistance, carrying communications between England and resistance groups in France. In early 1943, Peter Churchill was ordered back to London. While waiting for his plane, both agents were nearly caught by the Germans. They escaped, but had to move their activities 300 km north, to the mountains of the Haute-Savoie.

Members of the French Resistance use a machine gun to fire on German troops in the streets of Paris.

## Life in Ravensbrück

In May 1944, Odette was moved to Karlsruhe prison in Germany, and from there to the infamous Ravensbrück **concentration camp**. At first, she was kept in an underground room in complete darkness, with only a plank to sleep on. Then she was moved to a tiny cell, where she remained in isolation until the **Allies** liberated the camp in May 1945. Odette had been kept apart from people for over a year. But she never broke under the pressure or gave the Germans the secret information they wanted.

## Betrayal and capture

Odette and Peter started to work for the local resistance movement in their new area, but were betrayed by a **double agent**. They were captured by the Gestapo, the German secret police, and sentenced to death. To save Peter, Odette said that they were married and that she had forced him to come to France. She also claimed, more dangerously, to be a relative of the British prime minister, Winston Churchill. These lies may have prevented the two agents from being executed, but Odette was still tortured by the Gestapo. She refused to betray any of her resistance colleagues.

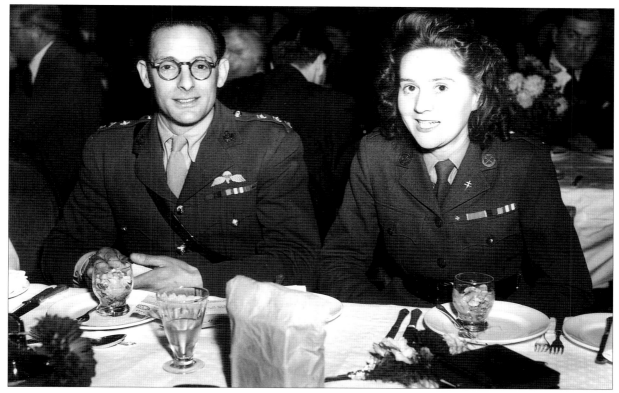

Odette and her future husband, Peter Churchill, shortly before their marriage in 1947.

## Ravensbrück concentration camp

Ravensbrück concentration camp for women was built 80 km north of Berlin, the German capital. It was set up in 1938 to hold 6000 inmates, but by the end of the Second World War, it housed more than 36 000.

From 1938 to 1945, over 50 000 women died in Ravensbrück, most as a result of harsh living conditions and punishing work. Some inmates were also injected with bacteria as part of a programme of medical experiments. They often died or became disabled.

One prisoner made sketches showing life in the camp. These have survived and give a vivid idea of what the inmates suffered (left).

## After the war

When the war was over, Odette was awarded the George Cross for her bravery, the highest award that a **civilian** can be granted. She also became very famous when books and a film celebrating her wartime activities were produced.

Odette's first husband had died during the war, so she married Peter Churchill. But the couple's peacetime marriage was not a success, and they soon divorced. In 1956, Odette got married a third time, to Geoffrey Hallowes.

Many ordinary people risked their lives in the resistance movements of occupied Europe. Some, like Odette Churchill, were horribly tortured by the enemy and yet never wavered in the fight for freedom.

# RAOUL WALLENBERG

**1912–?**

The most awful act to be carried out in the Second World War (1939-45) was the mass murder of Jews by the **Nazis**. This later became known as the Holocaust. Raoul Wallenberg was brave enough to help some Jews escape their terrible fate.

Wallenberg was born in Kappsta near Stockholm, Sweden, in 1912. His family were rich **Lutherans**. As a young man he studied architecture, then in 1936 became the foreign representative of a Central European trading company. Its president was a Hungarian Jew. Wallenberg worked hard for the company, and in 1939 made many business trips to Germany, France and Hungary. He was a respected figure, especially in Budapest, Hungary's capital.

## Nazi invasion

In March 1944, the Nazis sent troops into Hungary. The Germans had invaded mainly because they wanted to take the 700 000 Jews living there to **concentration camps**. Wallenberg was trusted by the Jewish community. So the Swedish and American governments, along with Jewish groups such as the World Jewish Congress and the American War Refugee Board, persuaded him to work undercover in order to save some of the Hungarian Jews.

Raoul Wallenberg, a Swedish businessman whose bravery saved up to 100 000 Jews.

## Adolf Eichmann

Adolf Eichmann joined the Nazi party as a young man and in 1942 was made responsible for the 'Final Solution'. This was the Nazi term for the mass execution of all European Jews. As a result of his plans, many Jews died in concentration camps (above). At the end of the Second World War in 1945, Eichmann escaped to Argentina. In 1958, **Israel**'s secret agents arrested him. He was put on trial, found guilty, and hanged on 31 May 1962.

## Rescue plans

Wallenberg's plan was to issue Jews with Swedish passports and to shelter them in protected houses, which flew the Swedish flag. As Sweden was **neutral** during the war, the Germans could not act against it. Wallenberg operated from the Swedish embassy in Budapest, with a staff that grew from 20 to over 600 at the end of the war. His department was called 'Section C'.

## Saving the Jews

Through secret meetings with officials, and by using bribes and threats, Wallenberg managed to save up to 100 000 Jews. He also went to stations where Jews were being **deported**, and distributed food and clothing. Other Jews were given money and official papers so that they could leave.

German troops deport a crowd of Hungarian Jews from the city of Budapest in 1944.

The Russian assault on Budapest in early 1945. Shortly afterwards, Wallenberg was taken prisoner.

## Heroic work

Wallenberg's heroic undercover work on behalf of the Jews, especially those living in the Budapest **ghetto**, won him an international reputation. He was often threatened by the Nazis. But because Wallenberg was a citizen of a neutral country, they did not dare to interfere.

## Arrest by the Soviets

Wallenberg's work was brought to a tragic end not by the Nazis, but by the Soviets. In January 1945, Soviet troops entered Budapest to liberate the city, and Wallenberg asked them to support his rescue missions. But his papers, radio and unusual activities made the Soviets think that he was an American spy. They arrested him, then took him to Soviet headquarters. He never returned.

This is the last known photograph of Wallenberg. He sent it to his mother on 26 November 1944.

## A great mystery

The mystery of Raoul Wallenberg started to grow. The Swedish authorities claimed that the Soviets had admitted his arrest was a mistake during a confused period at the end of the war, and that he had died of a heart attack in Moscow's Lubyanka Prison in 1947. But there were other, unconfirmed reports that Wallenberg had been seen alive in prison in 1951, 1959 and 1975.

## Honorary citizen

On 22 September 1981, the USA granted Raoul Wallenberg honorary citizenship. Israel granted him the same honour in 1986, and a tree was planted there in his memory (see below). Tragically, we may never know what happened to Wallenberg. But many thousands of people owe him their lives, and he is certainly one of the bravest undercover agents of all time.

### Yad Vashem

Yad Vashem is Hebrew for 'lasting memorial'. This is the name of the monument established in Jerusalem in 1953 to preserve the memory of the Jews exterminated by Nazi Germany. The road leading up to it is known as the Avenue of the Righteous, and trees are planted there to commemorate non-Jews who risked their lives to save Jews. In 1986, a tree to honour Wallenberg was planted there (right).

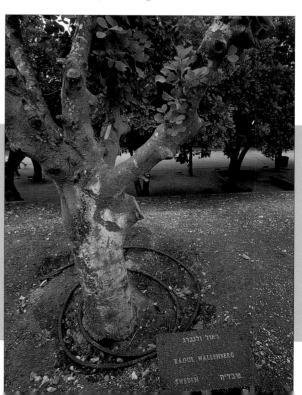

# GLOSSARY

**Alias** A false name.

**Allies** The countries that fought Germany together in the Second World War.

**Appeasement** The 1930s policy of attempting to keep the peace with Germany by giving in to its demands.

**Austro-Hungarian Empire** The empire of Austria and the kingdom of Hungary combined. It lasted from 1867 to 1918.

**Bavaria** A former state, today an administrative region, in south Germany.

**Black-out** A sudden loss of consciousness.

**Blockade** A ring of troops around a city.

**British Expeditionary Force** The first British troops sent to mainland Europe during the Second World War.

**Chandler** A candle-maker and seller.

**Chief of Staff** The senior officer of each of the armed forces.

**Civilian** A person not in the armed forces.

**Cold War** The political conflict between the USA and the Soviet Union during the 1950s and 1960s.

**Communist** A supporter of Communism, which states that all people are equal and property should not be privately owned.

**Concentration camp** A place in which large numbers of people are held by force and often inhumanly treated.

**Constitution** The laws according to which a country is governed.

**Cossack** A member of a people from south-east Russia who served as cavalry soldiers during times of war.

**Cotton gin** A machine for separating the seeds of cotton from the fibres.

**Court-martial** A military court where offences against military law are tried.

**Creditor** A person, group or country to whom money is owed.

**Custody** The right to keep a child in one's home and to be its main carer.

**Deport** To remove from a country.

**Divine right** The belief that monarchs' right to rule comes from God.

**Double agent** A person who spies for two opposing powers at the same time.

**Draft** To make a person join the army.

**Druggist** A chemist.

**Federation** A group of states that act separately on internal issues, such as education, but together on foreign policy.

**French and Indian War** (1754-63) A war between France and Britain that was fought in North America.

**Führer** The title taken by Adolf Hitler. It is German for 'leader'.

**Ghetto** An area in a town where one group of people lives apart from others.

**Guerrilla** A fighter who wages war by ambush and surprise attack.

**Hanged, drawn and quartered** Hanged, cut open to remove the bowels, then chopped into pieces.

**Hosiery** Knitted stockings and socks.

**Idol** A statue worshipped as a god.

**Intelligence** Secret service members.

**Israel** The independent Jewish republic established in the Middle East in 1948.

**Libel** Publication of a statement that damages the reputation of a person or organization.

**Lonely hearts** Unattached people who advertise for a marriage partner.

**Lutheran** A person who believes in the religious doctrines of Martin Luther.

**Military honours** Signs of respect displayed by troops, such as saluting.

**Militia** A private army.

**Nazi** A follower of the German National Socialist movement led by Adolf Hitler.

**Neutral** Not allied to either side in a war.

**Pillory** A wood frame with holes in which a criminal's head and hands are locked.

**Protestant** A follower of the branch of Christianity that broke away from Roman Catholicism at the Reformation.

**Rack** An instrument of torture that stretches the body, causing extreme pain.

**Reformation** The sixteenth-century European movement that aimed to reform the Roman Catholic Church.

**Resistance** An organization working against (resisting) an occupying army.

**Roman Catholic** A member of the Roman Catholic Church, which is led by the Pope in Rome.

**Slav** A member of a group of peoples living in Eastern Europe that includes Russians, Poles and the peoples of the former Yugoslavia.

**Subversion** Activities designed to overthrow governments.

**Telegraph** An instrument that transmits electrical impulses along wires as a means of sending messages.

**Yeomen of the Guard** Soldiers who act as the British monarch's bodyguards.

# INDEX